T0061057

DYNAMITE EXPLODE

T CHAMPIONSHIP OF THE WORLD

XING

NIGHT

EVENT- 10 ROUNDS

EATEST OF ALL TIME !

To the Champion, Muhammad Ali —J. H.

For my dad, Chu, who loves boxing —E. V.

First published in the United States of America in May 2002
by Walker Books for Young Readers, an imprint of Bloomsbury Publishing, Inc.
New edition published in January 2018 by Bloomsbury Children's Books
www.bloomsbury.com

Bloomsbury is a registered trademark of Bloomsbury Publishing Plc

For information about permission to reproduce selections from this book, write to
Permissions, Bloomsbury Children's Books, 1385 Broadway, New York, New York 10018
Bloomsbury books may be purchased for business or promotional use. For information on bulk purchases
please contact Macmillan Corporate and Premium Sales Department at specialmarkets@macmillan.com

The Library of Congress has cataloged the original edition as follows:
Haskins, James.
Champion : the story of Muhammad Ali / Jim Haskins ; illustrations by Eric Velasquez.
p.   cm.
Summary: A biography of Muhammad Ali, from his childhood in Louisville, Kentucky, his legendary boxing career, and his
conversion to Islam and opposition to the war in Vietnam, to his appearance at the 1996 summer Olympics in Atlanta.
ISBN 0-8027-8784-3 (hardcover) • ISBN 0-8027-8785-1 (rein)
1. Ali, Muhammad, 1942—Juvenile literature. 2. Boxers (Sports)—United States—Biography—Juvenile literature.
[1. Ali, Muhammad, 1942– 2. Boxers (Sports) 3. African Americans—Biography.] I. Velasquez, Eric, ill. II. Title.
GV1132.A44.H36   2001   796.83'092—dc21   [B]   2001045374

ISBN 978-1-68119-588-9 (new edition) • ISBN 978-1-68119-854-5 (e-book) • ISBN 978-1-68119-855-2 (e-PDF)

Illustrations painted in oil on Fabriano paper
Book design by Jeanette Levy
Printed in China by Leo Paper Products, Heshan, Guangdong
10 9 8 7 6 5

CHAMPION

THE STORY OF
MUHAMMAD
ALI

JIM HASKINS

ILLUSTRATED BY

ERIC VELASQUEZ

BLOOMSBURY

NEW YORK LONDON OXFORD NEW DELHI SYDNEY

MUHAMMAD ALI was riding in an airplane one time. Although he didn't like flying, he realized it gave him a special view of the world. He looked out the window and down to the earth below him. "I could hitchhike around the world," he thought. No matter where he was, someone would know him. Someone would feed him. Someone would give him a place to sleep. He was probably the most famous person alive.

He was the heavyweight boxing champion of the world. Some said he was the greatest boxer in history. Everyone said he was the fastest. He was more than that. He was a new kind of boxer. He had helped change the image of professional boxing from a brutal pastime to a widely popular sport. He also had shown the world that he could be true to himself and his beliefs and still be a winner.

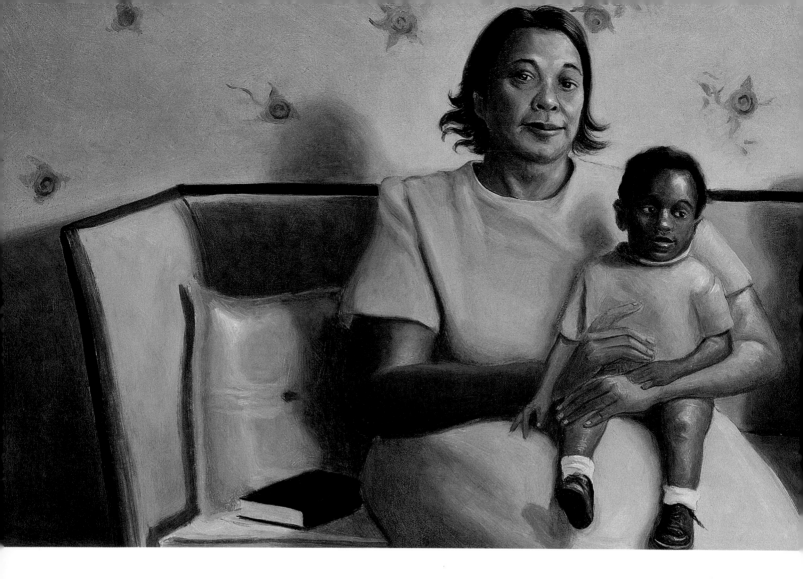

MUHAMMAD ALI was born on January 17, 1942, in Louisville, Kentucky. He was named Cassius Marcellus Clay Jr., after his father. He was also named after a nineteenth-century white plantation owner who had freed all his slaves and worked to end slavery. Cassius Jr.'s great-grandfather had grown up on that first Cassius Clay's land in Kentucky.

Cassius's father was a sign painter who loved to talk and make jokes. Cassius began to talk at a young age and also liked to make jokes.

His mother, Odessa Clay, earned money for food by cooking and cleaning for white people. She was very religious. She read the Bible every day and took Cassius and his brother, Rudy, to church every Sunday.

Cassius grew up in a time when blacks were forced to stay apart from whites. He and Rudy had to go to a school for blacks. Like most other blacks in Louisville then, the Clays were quite poor. There was no school bus for black kids, and the Clays didn't have enough money to pay public bus fare for both boys. So they usually had to walk to and from school. Young Cassius announced that he wanted to be rich one day, but his father told him he could never be rich because his skin was not white. Although he was basically a happy child, Cassius sometimes cried himself to sleep over what his people had to suffer.

FOR his twelfth birthday, Cassius received a shiny red bicycle. It was stolen almost as soon as he got it. Cassius wanted to find the thief and beat him up. A policeman told Cassius that he had better learn how to fight first. Cassius never got his bike back. He got a mission in life instead.

The policeman ran a gym. He offered to teach Cassius to box. Cassius decided that boxing as a sport was more important than fighting in anger. He learned that there were many famous black boxers. In fact, there were more black boxers in the United States than there were white boxers. Boxing was a way he could become rich and famous. He went to the gym every chance he got. He ate and drank only healthy things. He began running five miles every morning. He also started racing the bus to school.

CASSIUS got better and better at boxing. He had quick reflexes. While he was in junior high and high school, Cassius fought in amateur bouts. Talkative and funny, he started predicting in what round of the fight he would knock out his opponents. He made up silly poems to tell reporters when they interviewed him. One went like this:

> " **This guy must be done—**
> **I'll stop him in one.** "

By the time he was
eighteen, he had won
one hundred amateur
fights, including
four national boxing
championships. He had
lost only eight bouts.

IN 1960, the Summer Olympics were held in Rome, Italy. Cassius tried out and made the U.S. Olympic boxing team as a light heavyweight. He was so afraid of flying that he bought his own parachute in an army surplus store and wore it on the flight to Rome.

Cassius fought four Olympic bouts. He beat fighters from Australia, Belgium, Poland, and Russia to win the Olympic gold medal. He was so proud of that medal that he wore it to bed at night.

Back at home, his father painted the front steps of the house red, white, and blue. The city of Louisville gave Cassius a hero's welcome. Cassius recited a special poem for the occasion, making reference to a figure in Roman history who was also named Cassius. It began:

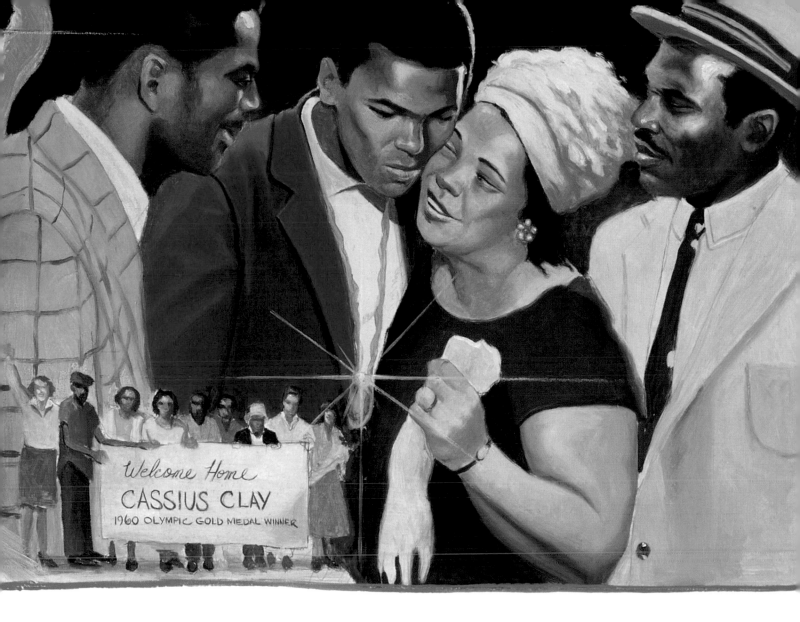

Welcome Home
CASSIUS CLAY
1960 OLYMPIC GOLD MEDAL WINNER

" To make America the greatest is my goal. . . .
And for the U.S.A. I won the Medal of Gold.
Italians said, 'You're greater than
the Cassius of Old.' "

NOT long afterward, Cassius Clay walked into a restaurant and ordered a glass of orange juice. The owner would not serve him because he was black. Cassius said that the pain he felt was like having to take punches without hitting back.

After the Olympics, Cassius turned professional. From then on, he fought for money. A group of local white businessmen paid his expenses. They hired a white boxing trainer named Angelo Dundee.

At six feet three inches tall and weighing almost two hundred pounds, Cassius was now a heavyweight boxer. He had the same quickness as when he was twelve. He also had the same loud mouth. People called him "The Louisville Lip" and "Blabber Mouth." He didn't care.

He bragged:

> **They all must fall
> In the round I call.**

IN 1964, Cassius went up against the heavyweight champion of the world. Sonny Liston was an ex-convict, backed by the mafia. Cassius boasted:

> **Sonny Liston is great
> But he'll fall in eight.**

Secretly, he was scared. Liston was older and bigger and a brutal fighter. Cassius knew he could get hurt. Sports reporters were predicting that he would be knocked out in the first round.

Cassius knew the only way he could beat Liston was to be smarter than him. One of his trainers said he would have to "float like a butterfly, sting like a bee." So Cassius danced around the bigger man. He dodged Liston's fists round after round. When he saw that Liston was getting tired, he started throwing punches. Many of them found their target. Liston refused to come out of his corner for round seven.

Cassius Clay was heavyweight champion of the world. Raising his arms in victory, he shouted,

**" I am the king!
I am the king! "**

THE day after he beat Sonny Liston, Cassius Clay made a surprising announcement. He was no longer a Christian. He was now a member of the Nation of Islam, also known as the Black Muslims. The Nation follows many of the beliefs of Islam but also emphasizes black pride. Unlike the segregation Cassius faced as a child, the Nation of Islam's separation was a form of black empowerment. Black Muslims often took new names to honor their Muslim faith, or as a sign that they rejected their place in white American society. Cassius Clay took a whole new Islamic name: Muhammad Ali.

Like Muslims all over the world, Muhammad Ali prayed five times a day. He also prayed in the boxing ring before every bout. He attended Nation of Islam temples and world Muslim mosques wherever he could find them. He married a Muslim woman. Officials of the Nation took over management of his boxing career, but Ali kept his white trainer, Angelo Dundee.

Over the next two years, Muhammad Ali defended his world title several times, fighting British, German, Canadian, and American opponents, including a rematch with Sonny Liston. He was at the top of his form, and he kept the world heavyweight title for a total of three years. There is no telling how long he would have remained champion.

IN 1967, the United States was deeply involved in the Vietnam War. U.S. troops were helping South Vietnam fight against the Vietcong of North Vietnam. Young men across the country were being called to serve in the army. Muhammad Ali refused to join the army, saying,

> **Keep asking me, no matter how long**
> **On the war in Viet Nam, I sing this song**
> **'I ain't got no quarrel with them Vietcong.'**

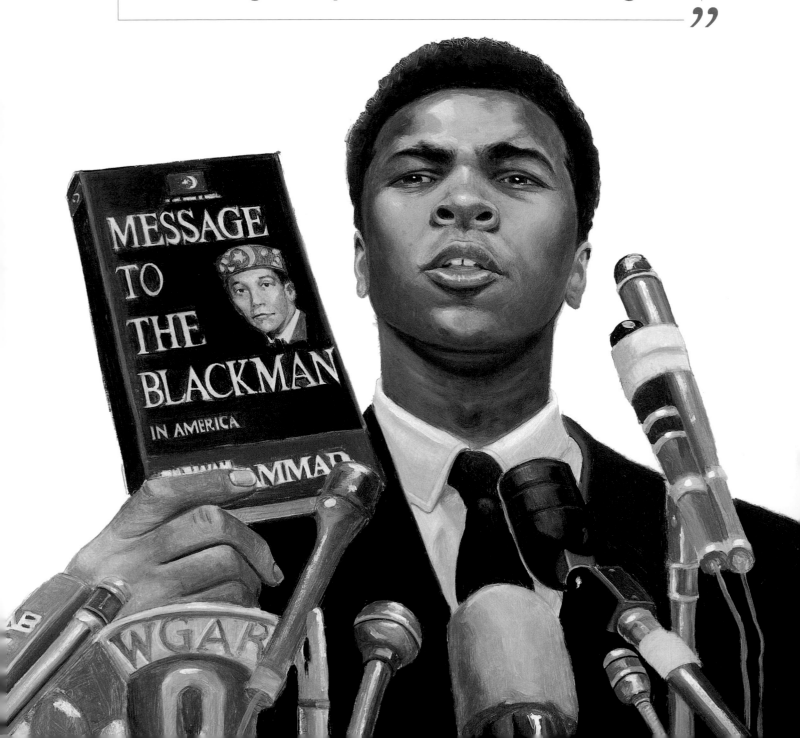

The United States had outlawed racial segregation while Ali was heavyweight champion of the world. But blacks were still denied many opportunities. Ali said he did not believe in fighting for freedom for other people when his own people were not free. Members of the Nation of Islam did not serve in the military. They did not get involved in politics or even vote.

The United States government charged him with the crime of refusing military service and prosecuted him for draft evasion. Ali was sentenced to pay a fine and spend five years in jail. He was allowed to remain free while he appealed the verdict to a higher court, but he was banned from boxing and his title was taken away from him.

THE ban was a terrible blow to Muhammad Ali's career. He did not have a professional boxing match for nearly four years. As other heavyweight boxers won and lost the championship, Ali insisted that the title was still his. Until someone beat him in the ring, he believed that he remained the true champion.

Ali spent his years of exile speaking out against the Vietnam War. During this difficult time, he drew strength from his faith. Islam had helped him overcome other challenges in the past. It helped him conquer his fear of flying and had enabled him to take his first trip to Africa, where there are many Muslims. Ali learned that other sects of Islam accept believers of all races, and he eventually converted to Sunni Islam.

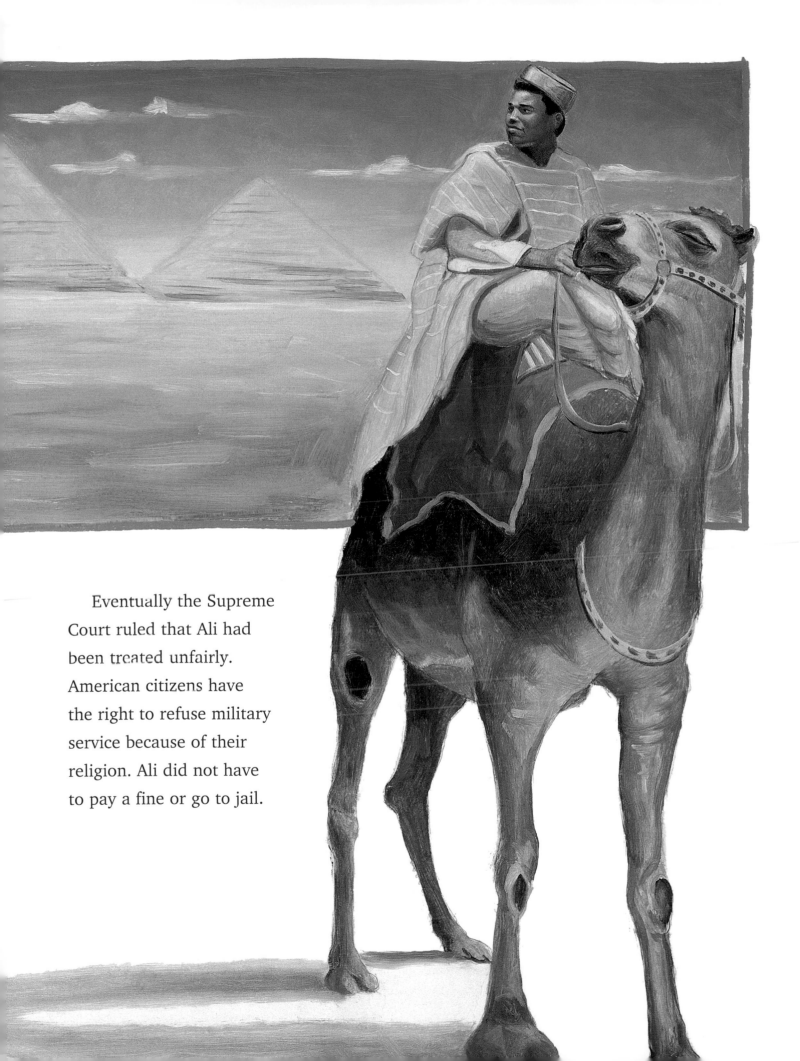

Eventually the Supreme Court ruled that Ali had been treated unfairly. American citizens have the right to refuse military service because of their religion. Ali did not have to pay a fine or go to jail.

ALI was nearly twenty-nine years old when he returned to boxing. He had lost some of his speed. Some people believed his days as a winner in the boxing ring were over. Ali proved them wrong, winning his first fight against Jerry Quarry by a knockout in the third round. By the time he went up against Argentine boxer Oscar Bonavena, he was writing poems again. His poem about the Bonavena fight ended with:

**Before Round Nine is out
The referee will jump and shout,
"THAT'S ALL, FOLKS,
this turkey is out!"**

vs. Quarry

vs. Bonavena

This time, his prediction did not come true. It took him fifteen rounds to knock out Bonavena.

On March 8, 1971, Ali went up against the world heavyweight champion Joe Frazier. Ali was almost knocked out, and the judges awarded the win to Frazier. It was the first loss of his professional career. Ali accepted the defeat, but he declared that he wanted to fight Frazier again.

Three years passed, and many of Ali's matches lasted much longer than they had when he was younger. He had his jaw broken in a fight against Ken Norton for his second loss.

Meanwhile, Joe Frazier lost the heavyweight title to George Foreman. Finally, the two ex-champions, Ali and Frazier, had their rematch. This time Ali outboxed Frazier. The judges awarded him the win. Now, Ali could go up against Foreman for the heavyweight boxing crown.

vs. Norton

vs. Frazier, 1974

BY 1974, Foreman had won all twenty-four of his professional fights by knockouts. Ali trained harder than he ever had before. The fight was staged in the African nation of Zaire and was billed as the "Rumble in the Jungle." It was a proud moment for all of black Africa, which was fighting against white South Africa's support of racism. Ali hoped it would be a proud moment for him. He knew it was going to be a tough fight. Foreman was younger and stronger. But Ali was faster and more experienced. He knocked down Foreman in the

eighth round, and the referee counted him out. After seven long years,
Muhammad Ali had won his title back.

During those years, Ali had also won respect. Most Americans had come to
believe that the United States was wrong to fight in Vietnam. They admired
Ali for standing up to the government. They also understood that he was
sincere in his religious faith. He had not tried to escape the draft by using
religion as an excuse. He remained a devoted follower of Islam.

ALI wanted to retire from boxing before he was seriously injured. He believed that his style of fighting protected him. As he put it in one of his poems:

> " **In the ring I can stay**
> **Until I'm old and gray**
> **Because I know how to hit**
> **And dance away.** "

His style depended on speed, however, and he was slowing down. Although he won many bouts, he was injured several times. His third and final bout in

1975 against Joe Frazier in the Philippines, known as "The Thrilla in Manila," is considered by many to be the greatest boxing match of all time. Ali won, but at great cost. He took nearly 440 punches during that one fight.

In 1978, after defending his title successfully ten times, he lost it to Leon Spinks. He regained the title by beating Spinks seven months later and became the first boxer to win the heavyweight championship three times. He then announced his retirement.

He returned to the ring for two more bouts in 1980 and 1981 and lost both. At thirty-nine years old, he was beginning to suffer from brain damage. He looked the same, but he sometimes had trouble speaking. His reflexes were slowing and his movements could be stiff. He had an incurable condition called Parkinson's disease, which steadily eroded his control over his own body.

ALI spent most of his years in retirement with his family. He and his fourth wife, Lonnie, adopted a child, Assad. Ali spent time with him and his other eight children. They had many visitors and Ali did magic tricks to entertain them. He remained a devout Muslim and prayed five times a day. For the rest of his life, he considered himself the world's goodwill ambassador.

In 1996, Muhammad Ali made a surprise appearance at the Summer Olympics in Atlanta, Georgia. He was the final bearer of the torch that lights the Olympic flame and opens the games. His arm shook as he held the symbol of international sporting competition. No one had expected him, and the crowd in the stadium and the billions of television watchers throughout the world cheered with love and respect. Ali was as much a symbol himself as was the torch. He was a symbol of strength and skill, of courage and pride. He was a man who broke down barriers and who brought people together—a champion in more ways than one.

TIMELINE

1942
Born in Louisville, Kentucky, January 17

1959
Wins Golden Gloves Championship in Chicago

1960
Wins Olympic gold medal in Rome; turns professional

1973
Fights four times; has his jaw broken by Ken Norton, but wins the rematch

1972
Wins six fights, four by knockouts

1971
Loses to heavyweight champion Joe Frazier; five-year jail sentence reversed; wins three later fights

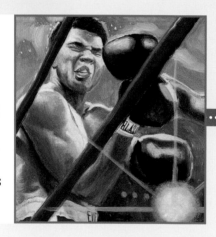

1975–78
After successfully defending his title ten times, loses heavyweight crown to Leon Spinks; beats Leon Spinks in rematch to regain heavyweight crown, the first boxer to win the crown three times

1979
Announces his retirement from boxing

1974
Beats Joe Frazier; knocks out George Foreman to reclaim the heavyweight boxing crown

1964

Beats Sonny Liston to become heavyweight champion of the world; announces his membership in the Nation of Islam

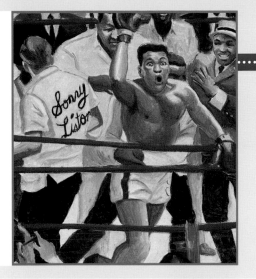

1965

Beats Liston in a rematch; defends his title against Floyd Patterson

1966

Wins five more fights, four by knockouts

1970

Regains his license and wins his first two fights

1967–70

Gives speeches against the Vietnam War at colleges during his ban from boxing

1967

Wins two more fights, one by knockout; refuses to be inducted into the army and is sentenced to five years in jail; his lawyers appeal the sentence; has his boxing license suspended

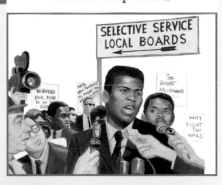

1980–81

Comes out of retirement; loses his last two bouts against Larry Holmes and Trevor Berbick

1996

Lights the torch to open the Olympic Games in Atlanta, Georgia

2016

Dies in Scottsdale, Arizona, June 3